ONE-MINUTE
LESSONS FOR LIFE

One-Minute Lessons For Life

An Essential Guide for Parents, Teachers & Mentors

Shana Alexander, Ed.M.

iUniverse, Inc.
New York Lincoln Shanghai

One-Minute Lessons For Life
An Essential Guide for Parents, Teachers & Mentors

iUniverse, Inc.

For information address:
iUniverse, Inc.
2021 Pine Lake Road, Suite 100
Lincoln, NE 68512
www.iuniverse.com

This publication is intended to provide educational
information for the reader on the covered subjects. It is not
meant to take the place of personalized counseling,
diagnosis, and treatment from a trained professional.

ISBN: 0-595-30507-5

Printed in the United States of America

To my parents, husband, and children.

Thank you.

*"Getting what you go after is success;
but liking it while you are getting it is happiness."*

Bertha Damon, 1943

Contents

*"How we spend our days is,
of course, how we spend our lives."*

Annie Dillard, 1989

Contents (continued)

*"The fragrance always remains in the hand
that gives the rose."*

Heda Bejar, 1989

Acknowledgments

I would like to offer special thanks to Thomas Rockwell for granting permission to make use of his father's classic artwork. Norman Rockwell's paintings capture the simple pleasures and pains of life with the same gentle honesty I strive to have in my words. Such generous support is empowering.

This book benefited enormously from the sound advice, genuine enthusiasm, and fine editorial skills of Dave, Linda, and Leanne. Additionally, the profound influence of Terry, Phyllis, and Gretchen will continue to impact my life long after the completion of this work.

I am still learning how much I appreciate the extraordinary examples provided by my parents. Their wisdom and uncommon devotion to family continues to serve as a guide to me. I also gain insight and inspiration from my sisters, close friends, and extended family around the country. Thank you, each of you.

This book is a guide for me as much as for anyone else. It was inspired by an intense desire to pass on the sense of security and happiness my husband and children have bestowed upon me. They are my reason for learning and my incentive for teaching. God bless you, family.

To all individuals who resolve to actively teach young people skills that will lead them in the direction of life-long happiness and success, thank you.

"Luck is a matter of preparation meeting opportunity."

Oprah Winfrey

Introduction

I was driving home from school contemplating how I might curtail a phenomenon that was sweeping over the girls in my fifth grade class. Apparently an older cousin had taken two of my students to a Britney Spears concert over the weekend. Now, I was finding clip-on bellybutton rings on the floor, sparkle make-up in the bathroom, and their clothing was getting skimpier by the day. Pop culture had declared war on my classroom and schoolwork was losing the battle.

Although I had spent hours preparing it, my lesson on the Aztec Indians didn't stand a chance. These girls didn't want to hear about anything older than last month's *Teen* magazine. And the boys were completely caught up in watching the girls' bizarre behavior and wondering where they fit into the picture. Even if I *could* get them to complete their assignments, which was no easy effort, I knew they were just going through the motions for the grade.

I was staring at a red light when the thought entered my mind. Forget the fifth-grade educational curriculum guide for a moment and suppose I could teach these kids anything: **What would I share with them if my sole intent was to give them the information they would need to create lasting success and happiness in their lives?** On the back of an envelope I started to make a list. Then, somebody beeped their horn behind me and I took off in the direction of home.

I hit the door running for the computer and didn't get up until I had an inventory of approximately eighty skills all children and teenagers should be taught. I started looking for ways to further categorize this seemingly random collection of ideas. Quite naturally, they divided into four lists: personal values, physical health, communication, and academic skills. I then started to reflect on the most essential things an individual should know for each topic. Within a few weeks an outline had developed.

With the permission of the principal, I worked some of these concepts into my classroom lessons. One that was especially well received by Britney fans and parents alike was an analysis of the marketing techniques used by the artist's management people. After the kids got over the initial shock that Ms. Spear's image was created specifically for the purpose of making millions of dollars every year, her allure was tarnished and they became savvy advertising sleuths. Collectively, they listed forty-five separate products and ideas that were sold using her image. One cooperative group went as far as to "star" the items that specifically targeted girls under the age of thirteen.

The environment of the classroom slowly evolved from an immature, begging-for-their-attention atmosphere to the site of student-motivated quests for knowledge. Suddenly, they wanted to know about all things real. Whether it was what happens to your money when you put it in the bank or how to prepare vegetarian tacos, they could not get enough of it! I even explained in no uncertain terms exactly *why* it is moderately valuable, if not essential, to learn about the living habits of the Aztec Indians.

The summer came and I decided to take this outline one step further by developing each idea listed. However, knowing exactly how much time parents, teachers, and mentors have for reading pages and pages of detailed text, I limited myself to one page per topic. **This approach would enable adults to easily introduce and discuss one page a day with their child or children.** Finally, the checklist format would provide a well-deserved feeling of accomplishment.

It is my sincere hope that, above all, the reader takes away a sense of calm in acquiring this philosophy of teaching. Recognizing that it is entirely possible to teach an individual specifically *how* to create a happy and successful life is exhilarating. And having a simple four-part framework to follow in introducing these skills is empowering. Children and teenagers love to learn about real life and following this direct teaching method gives them not only what they desire, but also what they need. Share *One-Minute Lessons For Life* today and you will enjoy sharing in their success tomorrow.

Shana Alexander

Chapter 1

Personal Values

*"Happiness is not something you get,
but something you do."*

Marcelene Cox, 1947

Happiness

☐ *Most likely to succeed.* Successful people are not necessarily those who get perfect grades and high-paying jobs. Individuals who make smart choices and use common sense to actively pursue and share happiness in life are most successful in the end.

☐ *Balance-it's not just for bicycles!* If you are having a bad day, week, or year, most likely a part of your life is getting too much or too little attention. Extreme amounts of work, money, stress, food, and "stuff" can result in problems. Make changes to maintain your equilibrium and *enjoy the ride.*

☐ *Enjoy today.* From a very young age we look forward to our next birthday until suddenly we start to look back—longingly. At least twice a day, STOP and enjoy a pleasant sight, sound, or experience. It is smart to learn from the past and plan for the future, but not at the sacrifice of today.

☐ *Satisfaction guaranteed.* Clever advertising campaigns create an endless sense of dissatisfaction in an effort to sell products and services. Don't buy it. Learning how to feel content with what you have and who you are is the only way to "guarantee" true satisfaction.

Simplicity p. 13, Generosity p. 23, Respect p. 25

"People tend to forget their duties but remember their rights."

Indira Gandhi, 1984

Responsibility

❏ *Good news, bad news.* The "sue happy" nature of our society has dramatically increased safety standards throughout the United States. However, the bad news is a decline in a sense of personal responsibility. Learning to accept the consequences of your decisions and behaviors boosts self-respect and earns it from others.

❏ *Increased maturity should precede increased responsibility.* There are 10-year-old children who can wash their own clothes and 20-year-old adults who cannot. Maturity is not defined by age; it is a result of explicit teaching. Age-appropriate expectations, directions, and consistent consequences result in responsible people.

❏ *Think for yourself.* Many people are more likely to live with purple hair than to disagree with what their beautician recommends. More serious results can occur when a doctor, auto mechanic, or financial advisor gives faulty advice. Responsible individuals ask questions, educate themselves, and draw their own conclusions.

❏ *Will power will give you power.* Self-control may be a foreign concept to those who have never had boundaries imposed upon them. They grow up with the false impression that their every wish should, and will, be granted. Reality can be a rude awakening. Learn how to resist over-indulgence and you will feel strong.

Parenthood p. 103, Education p. 119, Insurance p. 123

"I go where I love and where I am loved."

H.D., 1946

Love

❑ *"I love you" does not replace "I like you."* If you would not speak to a friend or a colleague in a certain manner, the same goes for those we love. Compliment them behind their backs. Greet each other warmly on the telephone. Use their given name. Those we love deserve our friendship, too.

❑ *"I would die for you."* Thank you, but would you do the dishes? Long-lasting love is infinitely practical, dependable, and thoughtful. Verbal support is more precious than jewelry, time is more valuable than toys, laughter is more important than expensive vacations. And volunteering for kitchen duty—well, that's priceless.

❑ *Love is patient, love is kind.* Love is consistently holding children responsible for their own behavior. Love is giving sincere compliments and gentle criticism. Love is feeling happy with yourself so you can share it with others. Love is slowing down enough to listen. Love is not always the easy thing, but it is always the right thing.

❑ *A mother's wisdom* for her daughter, "A man who shows kindness toward children, animals, and his mother is capable of great love." Look for these traits in yourself and in others.

Dating p. 95, Marriage p. 99, Family p. 115

"Sex outside of marriage is like playing chicken with a train. If you do not want to get hit…GET OFF THE TRACKS!"

Georgia Ryan, 2003

Abstinence

☐ *Reality does not sell...*but the glamorous sex found in most magazines and on television does. Consequently, surgically enhanced models and sexual innuendoes are used to promote everything from toys to shampoo. The reality of sex outside of marriage is fear of broken promises, unwanted pregnancy, and disease.

☐ *Bad choices can happen to good people.* A 16-year-old girl gets pregnant because she didn't intend on having sex, "it just happened." A young man must live with herpes for the rest of his life even though he didn't "go all the way." Reserve sexual activity for the marriage of two people who are dedicated to one another.

☐ *Patience is growing in popularity.* It may not be the talk of the locker room, but the number of young people who want to avoid the negative effects of premature sexual activity is growing dramatically. They get involved in extracurricular activities and choose friends who will help them meet this goal.

☐ *"Virginity" is a purity of mind*, not only body. In other words, if an individual engages in every sexual act except intercourse, they are still at risk of sexually transmitted diseases, a damaged self worth, and unprepared intercourse. However, it also means a person can renew a pure sense of self after realizing a mistake and *taking action* to prevent it from happening again.

Puberty p. 45, Pregnancy p. 57, Dating p. 95

"The secret to happiness is not in getting more but in wanting less."

Elaine St. James

Simplicity

❑ *The history of stuff.* The Great Depression of the 1930s required saving and reusing nearly everything. The 1950s brought prosperity and a television set for most living rooms. Dual incomes during the 1980s resulted in three car garages brimming with stuff. Today, people are recognizing that less can be more.

❑ *Official definition of clutter-*75% of the stuff found in most clothing closets, kitchen drawers, garages, desks, and hard drives. Save money, make cleaning easy, enjoy what you have, and increase efficiency…get rid of and resist re-accumulating clutter. The first step toward organizing anything is in the direction of the recycle bin.

❑ *Maintenance is the key* to any organization system. A cardboard box can be just as effective as an expensive file cabinet if you keep up with it. Make a logical "home" for the useful items you keep after simplifying your living spaces. And when you are finished reading, playing, using, wearing, or watching it, put it away!

❑ *Too much of a good thing.* Relationships, careers, hobbies, education, family, faith, and social life can often benefit from a thorough prioritization and simplification. Do a few activities with energy and enthusiasm, rather than just doing endless activities.

Generosity p. 23, Organization p. 153, Time Mgmt. p. 157

"A thorough conviction that nobody can get there unless everybody gets there."

Virginia Burden Tower, 1975

Cooperation

☐ *Create a single mission statement.* Compose one succinct sentence that encompasses the underlying purpose or final destination of a group's effort. Then, come to an agreement on the specific objectives and a schedule to meet the goal. When people know where they are going, they get there.

☐ *The rule of roles:* Members of successful families, corporations, and governments have a keen understanding of their rights and responsibilities within the organization. They receive credit for a job well done and they are held accountable for shortcomings.

☐ *Training.* A classroom that operates smoothly even when the teacher is absent is a class that has been well taught. A soccer team that changes old habits to win the game is a team well coached. Success is a learned behavior. It is the result of specific training and practice.

☐ *Too many cooks.* There are times when committees, councils, and cooperative efforts can make a relatively simple job more complicated. Sometimes it is wise to give more responsibility and resources to a single motivated individual who can complete the assignment effectively and efficiently.

Leadership p. 21, Conversation p. 83, Disagreement p. 93

*"Ask not what this country can do for you—
ask what you can do for your country."*

John F. Kennedy, 1961

Nationalism

❑ *July 4, 1776.* Honor those who have died fighting for freedom and respect those who defend it today. The United States military has provided a way of life we must never take for granted. Show your appreciation often in word and in deed because, for Americans, Independence Day is every day.

❑ *E Pluribus Unum.* New immigrants to America should feel free to maintain many of the cultural traditions of their homeland, as they gradually find their place within American culture. It is critical, however, that newcomers are encouraged to become loyal U.S. citizens because only *united will we stand.*

❑ *Sea to shining sea.* American topography is as diverse as our society. Experience the rugged mountains, oceans of wheat, sun-soaked coastlines, racing city life, and quiet rural countryside. Enjoy the accents, taste the foods, and learn the traditions of our American culture.

❑ *Help wanted.* Considering the educational, financial, and even personal well-being of every citizen is routine for the United States Government. Few countries in the world are so fortunate. Individuals should recognize and participate in this effort whenever possible.

Cooperation p. 15, History p. 137, Social Studies p. 139

"I find to my astonishment that an unhappy marriage goes on being unhappy when it is over."

Rebecca West, 1987

Divorce

❏ *Desperately seeking successful marriages.* If your parents, siblings, neighbors, and coworkers are all divorced—BEWARE—bad habits are contagious. However, good ones are, too. Make a concerted effort to befriend couples (often found at places of worship) who respect their spouse and believe in marriage.

❏ *Little put-downs, BIG mistake.* When apologies go unsaid, the other person is left looking for an opportunity for revenge, even if it is just a little verbal jab. Often, this cycle will continue until one day the relationship has turned icy. Warm up to the people you care about, build them up whenever possible.

❏ *Children will do as you do,* not as you say. This is something to keep in mind as you work hard to create a safe, respectful, and kind environment for them to grow up in. Address problems while they are small, make use of help resources, and consider the needs of children before those of adults.

❏ *There is no room for abuse* of any kind in your home. Every man, woman, and child is entitled to a safe haven to retreat to when they are happy, sad, well, or sick. If your house is not this place, get help. Get help. Get help.

Disagreement p. 93, Marriage p. 99, Help p. 101

"Be the change you wish to see in the world."

Gandhi

Leadership

❏ *Sometimes you lead,* sometimes you follow. No one person is ideally qualified for all positions of management. A four-star general may be at a loss in a kindergarten classroom, for example. Look for related experience, education, personal dedication, and communication skills when choosing a person to manage your cause.

❏ *Explain why.* There is value in training personnel to follow orders without question, especially in times where safety is at risk. However, subordinates often feel more dedicated to an effort when they understand *why* they are doing *what* they are doing. Do not assume the ultimate goal for a course of action is obvious.

❏ *A boss is not a buddy.* A manager needs to be able to do what is necessary to achieve success without being excessively concerned with popularity. However, effective leaders also support creating a positive work environment and recognize the value of team solidarity.

❏ *The wind beneath their wings.* Intelligent leaders never let their often-visible position go to their heads. A coach would not be able to manage a successful soccer team without the support of the players, parents, and community members. Smart leaders emphasize the value of all of the contributors.

Cooperation p. 15, Confidence p. 77, Organization p. 153

"I don't want you to give me your surplus.
I want you to give with personal deprivation."

Mother Teresa, 1977

Generosity

❑ *Children between birth and three years of age* are expected to believe the world revolves around them; the rest of us have no excuse. Look at the people in your family, community, country, and world. Consider their situation and feelings when you are evaluating your own. Empathy is the first step toward generosity.

❑ *No strings attached.* Generosity is not giving an expensive gift because it is expected. It is not volunteering because you feel guilty or are unable to say "no." It has nothing to do with rewards or self-gratification. Generosity is sharing your time, talent, and money anonymously, with an inner smile.

❑ *Accepting kindness is as important as giving it.* Many people feel far more comfortable giving than receiving. To accept a thoughtful gift allows another to feel the satisfaction that accompanies benevolence. When it is appropriate, take the gift with grace and a simple, sincere "thank you."

❑ *Adopt an attitude of gratitude.* It is easy to get caught up in complaining about frivolous things when we become complacent with our lives of plenty. An excellent way to express appreciation for the gifts in your life is to share them. You will find the more thankful you are, the more you have to be thankful for.

Happiness p. 5, Spirituality p. 27, Talents p. 33

"Respect is not a gift; you have to earn it."

Unknown

Respect

❑ *You must respect yourself* before others will. Never put yourself down verbally or physically. Do not smoke, drink excessively, or otherwise injure your own body. Stand up tall, dress nicely, and look at people in the eye. Do what you say, say what you think, and think about the things that you do well.

❑ *Respect with reservation.* Respect should have little to do with race, religion, gender, age, sexual orientation, physical appearance, or financial status of a person. It has everything to do with the thoughts, actions, and words of an individual. Those who are honest, fair, and kind earn the respect of others. Those who are not—do not.

❑ *Hide and seek.* When people grow up in homes where respect is not the norm, they honestly may not know *how* to show appreciation for others. However, they *will* suffer the consequences of this lack of education. Resist the temptation to put others down in an effort to build yourself up and respect will find you.

❑ *R.E.S.P.E.C.T.* From birth, children must be taught specifically *how* to show regard for themselves, their parents, their teachers, their friends, their belongings, their home, the property of others, animals, and nature. When it comes to respect and young people; demonstrate it for them, expect it from them, and give it to them.

Presentation p. 79, Body Language p. 87, Education p. 119

*"Religion is a bridge to the spiritual,
but the spiritual lies beyond religion."*

Rachel Naomi Remen, 1990

Spirituality

❑ *Lesson #1.* Young people who have a strong sense of character make wise decisions in life. They respect themselves enough to protect their physical health, learn to communicate effectively, and dedicate time and effort to achieving academic success. In other words, instill personal values in children and the rest will fall into place.

❑ *Faith life begins* as an individual journey. Sharing your convictions with others is a wonderful extension, but do not forget to focus on your own spiritual growth. Ask questions, reflect on answers, and apply what you learn to your everyday life. Because faith life also *ends* as an individual journey.

❑ *"Do unto others as you would have them do unto you."* No matter what religion you choose, most faiths simply ask people to be kind and good to one another above all else. Attending a church, synagogue, mosque, or temple often provides education and social support to help us keep this "Golden Rule."

❑ *Four steps to the perfect prayer:* (1) Thank you…. (2) I'm sorry…. (3) Please…. (4) Shhh…. Prayer is a conversation, so do not do all of the talking. At a quiet time, try to clear your mind of the things you know and feel, and be open to listening to the whispers of God.

Love p. 9, Leadership p. 21, Friendship p. 91

"What delights us in visible beauty is the invisible."

Marie von Ebner-Eschbach, 1893

Beauty

☐ *Accentuate the positive,* not just the popular. Instead of trying to change your features, make the most of what you have. There are beauty opportunities for every shape, color, texture, and size. Looking good is always popular, but what is "popular" does not always look good.

☐ *Secret weapon:* Confidence! Physical appearance is intimately tied to presentation skills. Spend the money, time, and effort you would otherwise use on physical enhancement and invest in learning how to depict self-assurance. Admirers will follow at every turn, no matter what your hair looks like.

☐ *Pretty perfect.* In an effort to sell literally billions of beauty products every year, marketing campaigns have convinced most people that no matter how attractive their hair, face, or bodies actually are, they *should* be better. Do what is necessary to *feel good* about your self and then—feel good!

☐ *Inner beauty is always "in."* From the beginning of time, people throughout the world have been obsessed with physical appearance. As a result, it takes a continuous effort to remember to judge others and ourselves on more genuine features. A beautiful personality outshines a pretty face.

Confidence p. 77, Presentation p. 79, Body Language p. 87

"Remember, people will judge you by your actions, not your intentions. You may have a heart of gold— but so does a hard-boiled egg."

Unknown

Habits

❑ *Make a habit of success.* To quit a bad habit permanently, an individual must have a clear goal in mind, realistic expectations, something positive to fill the void, and help when necessary. Decide whether to abruptly discontinue the behavior completely, or gradually limit it until it is gone. Now, hurry up and stop.

❑ *Celebrate your success.* Too often we look up at the mountain left to climb instead of recognizing the distance already traveled. If you have cut back from a bag of potato chips a day to a serving, that's great! Acknowledge your progress and use it as an incentive to keep moving toward your goal.

❑ *Do not start* smoking cigarettes, drinking alcohol irresponsibly, using drugs illegally, or having sex outside of marriage. The question is not whether these habits will cause pain or not, but *how* much pain they will cause. Do not start and you will not have to try to stop after damage is done.

❑ *Don't fix it if it ain't broke.* Throughout life, one should always work on self-improvement inside and out because we all have weaknesses. However, be sure to give the "good stuff" fair recognition because we all have strengths, too.

Simplicity p. 13, Disease p. 61, Diet and Nutrition p. 63

"The only thing that happens overnight is recognition. Not talent."

Carol Haney, 1957

Talents

❑ *Everyone has a responsibility,* not just a talent. Be it highly visible or quietly discreet, discovering and using your gifts to influence the world in a positive way is what every human being is called to do. If you are doing the right thing, sometimes it will feel like work, but much of the time it will feel like play.

❑ *Look for role models.* They may be famous or obscure, close or distant, human or super-human. It may be the whole package, or a certain aspect of an individual that you admire. Follow their inspiration, not their mistakes. And, one day, you will become a role model for someone else.

❑ *Make your dreams a reality,* in a practical way. Do not let a talent go to waste just because Hollywood will not return your calls. There are numerous ways to apply musical, artistic, acting, or athletic skills on a smaller scale. Additionally, prioritizing love and family above money or fame will make you a lasting star.

❑ *A talent a day* will keep the doctor away. Even if it is only for a short part of the day, doing what makes you smile has tremendous psychological, social, and even physical benefits. People should approach discovering healthy, natural talents and personal interests with the same serious intent they would a job or a spouse.

Generosity p. 23, Relaxation p. 73, Career p. 125

"We cannot really love anybody with whom we never laugh."

Agnes Repplier, 1921

Laughter

❑ *Laugh more, live longer!* This simple, pleasant behavior stimulates the nervous system, increases oxygen intake, and improves vital signs over all. It may or may not add years to one's life, but laughter surely adds life to one's years.

❑ *What's so funny?* Friends, cartoons, kids, comic strips, books, parents, children, strangers, magazines, radio, comedians, spouses, animals, church, television, movies, greeting cards, your imagination. Turn them on and laugh out loud.

❑ *The glass is half-funny.* How do some stand-up comedians bring an audience to absolute tears with laughter? He or she finds the humor in everyday life and then over-emphasizes it with extraordinary timing and talent. We cannot all be comedians, but looking for the lighter side of life can often make the mundane more enjoyable.

❑ *Healthy humor doesn't hurt.* Laughter at the expense of someone else's pain is false joy. In reality, it creates tension. Everyone wonders when it will be his or her turn to be the victim. Choose your humor wisely, for it can display your insights or expose serious faults.

Happiness p. 5, Relaxation p. 73, Body Language p. 87

Chapter 2

Physical Health

"Health is not simply the absence of sickness."

Adelle Davis, 1954

Exercise

❑ *Move beyond the mirror.* Exercise can be reduced to sweaty primping when tight buns are the only source of motivation. During workouts, focus on the internal sense of satisfaction you are gaining instead of the external inches you are loosing. It is easier to work toward a goal that is higher than your waistline.

❑ *Eat, sleep, exercise,* and be merry. Nutritious meals provide the energy necessary for a strong workout. Regular exercise increases the chance of a productive day. An active day encourages peaceful sleep. And a well-rested person is more likely to prepare nutritious meals. Get on that cycle and ride!

❑ *The complete workout.* Stretching warms up the muscles and helps prevent injury. Aerobic movement for at least twenty minutes gets your heart rate up and burns fat calories. Weight training tones and strengthens muscles while improving metabolism. A little discipline can take you a long way toward health and happiness.

❑ *Those who sweat together stay together.* Exercise, formal or otherwise, is one of the single most important things you, your spouse, your kids, and your dog will do today. Commit to twenty minutes of strenuous activity *every* day and watch not only your body, but also your relationships, shape up.

Habits p. 31, Sports p. 43, Diet and Nutrition p. 63

*"Safety success is silent.
It is the consequences of unsafe actions that scream."*

Georgia Ryan, 2001

Safety

❑ *Stay in control.* Take responsibility for your own safety. It should be obvious that alcohol and drugs can compromise your control. However, a submissive attitude can be equally damaging. Do not allow others to easily influence you and never let someone else think *for* you. YOU look before YOU leap.

❑ *"Never point a weapon* at a person unless you intend to kill them," a chilling reminder of reality from one Vietnam veteran. Some of the greatest injustices imposed upon children are cartoons, video games, movies, toys and costumes that create the illusion that guns are toys. Teach them the truth or someone else may.

❑ *The sequence of self-defense for males and females:*
1st **Think:** Keep yourself out of dangerous situations.
2nd **Attention:** Call for "help," throw things, honk a car horn.
3rd **Run:** Get to a populated area, find help, or hide.
4th **Fight:** (last option) Target soft spots like eyes, and run.

❑ *Don't worry, be smart.* Crime has existed throughout history, although it is far more published and dramatized in current times. The most effective weapon against violence is knowledge, not fear. Learn how to be safe, teach how to be safe, and then turn off the nightly news, fold up the paper, and enjoy the rest life has to offer.

Responsibility p. 7, Driving p. 47, Emergency Skills p. 69

"It's time to raise a generation of participants, not another generation of fans."

Janice Kaplan, 1979

Sports

❑ *Perfect practice makes perfect.* Successful athletes repeat skills until they become instinctive. This can be very useful in building concentration and endurance *if* you are practicing the method correctly. In life and in sports, look for good coaches. They can tell where form and technique can be improved.

❑ *Time out.* High school athletic programs are terrific ways to provide exercise and a sense of belonging for teenagers. However, taken to an extreme, sport commitments can overtake time to study, participate in other social opportunities, and family time. Take time out for other meaningful activities.

❑ *Sportsmanship is a life skill.* There are winners and there are losers in sports. Teammates who support each other through success and defeat win every time. The others are missing the point no matter how often they score. Do not just choose a sport, choose a winning team.

❑ *Think outside the basket.* Basketball and other team sports are great in high school, but don't stop there. There are dozens of individual and outdoor sports that can also offer exercise and enjoyment far beyond graduation. Learn to ski, rock climb, golf, backpack, play tennis, kayak, bike, fish, scuba dive and keep on playing!

Cooperation p. 15, Exercise p. 39, Puberty p. 45

*"There are years that ask questions
and years that answer."*

Zora Neale Hurston, 1937

Puberty

❑ *Girl to woman.* Usually, between the ages of 9 and 14, girls go through puberty. Their breasts grow larger, their hips widen, they grow hair in their underarm and pubic areas, and they begin menstruating (their "period"). These young women can now become pregnant.

❑ *Boy to man.* Boys usually start puberty between the ages of 11 and 15. They grow more body and facial hair, their voices deepen, they experience more frequent erections, and have occasional spontaneous ejaculation or "wet dreams" while sleeping. These young men can now make a woman pregnant.

❑ *SEX!* It is critical that teens are given accurate information and numerous opportunities to ask questions about sex. Adults must not hesitate to *repeatedly* address the possible physical, emotional, and financial repercussions of pre-marital sexual activity (not including self-exploration, which is normal and not harmful).

❑ *Doing the hormone swing.* Regular exercise, a healthy diet, eight to ten hours of sleep a night, and confidence-building socializing (such as participating in a church youth group) will help steady hormones. Parents should provide struc-ture, boundaries, and safe opportunities for teenagers to exercise their independence.

Abstinence p. 11, Friendship p. 91, Dating p. 95

"Responsibility is the price every man must pay for freedom. It is to be had on no other terms."

Edith Hamilton, 1961

Driving

❑ *Sixteen can be sweet* when a new driver always: wears a seat belt, is not easily distracted by passengers, and *never* drives under the influence of alcohol or drugs. They should also pay for their own car (at least partially), gas, auto insurance, tune-ups, and any tickets. Age does not determine driving readiness, maturity does.

❑ *Before stepping on the gas,* make sure you have some. Running out of fuel is one of the most common and avoidable hazards some drivers trifle with regularly. Get in the habit of refilling the tank when it is *half*-empty and you will not get stuck vulnerable and irritated *half*-way to your destination.

❑ *Distracted drivers are dangerous.* They are changing the radio station, talking on a cell phone, lighting a cigarette, falling asleep, looking at the scenery, putting on make-up, eating a burger, angry with a boyfriend, rushing to work, and so on. A safe driver simply gives other drivers space and stays alert.

❑ *Fender bender procedures.* Use your safety sense; *never* stop in a deserted place or in fast traffic. There are worse things that can happen than a bent bumper. *Always* call the police, no matter how minor the accident. And for your records, write down the other person's license plate number, make of the car, and details of the incident.

Responsibility p. 7, Safety p. 41, Insurance p. 123

"Depression sits on my chest like a sumo wrestler."

Sandra Scoppettone, 1993

Depression

❑ *Your feelings are real.* Your problems may seem dwarfed when compared with the struggling economies of Third World nations. However, the daily trials of *all* individuals are often worthy of time and sometimes tears. Talk to someone you trust and actively seek solutions.

❑ *The fear factor.* Why do some people stay in a bad relationship, endure a demeaning job, or refuse to take steps to escape loneliness? Solutions usually require change and many people would rather swim with sharks than endure transition—even if it is for the better. Create a plan, charge up your courage, get help if necessary, and DO it!

❑ *How are your hormones?* It may not be the most common question you hear, but perhaps it should be. Hormone stability affects how individuals of all ages sleep, eat, work, and interact with people. Depression, due to chemical or hormonal imbalance, is a very common and treatable condition. Talk to your doctor.

❑ *PMS anyone?* Gloominess and negativity can become a nasty habit. If you are suffering from Poor Me Syndrome (not to be confused with legitimate cases of premenstrual syndrome), then give yourself and everyone around you a break. Life looks better when you see it with a smile.

Generosity p. 23, Laughter p. 35, Exercise p. 39

*"Always buy a good bed and a good pair of shoes.
If you're not in one, you're in the other."*

Gloria Hunniford

Sleep

❑ *"Goodnight"* is the first step to a good day. Healthy sleep is as important to the human body as good nutrition and regular exercise. With it, you feel physically refreshed and mentally invigorated, without it, you…don't.

❑ *Irritable, lethargic, or unable to focus?* Too much or too little sleep can have similar negative side effects. The average amount of sleep required by babies is 15-20 hours daily, toddlers & children 10-12 hours, teen-agers 9-10 hours (most get about six), adults 7-9 hours and seniors 9-10 hours.

❑ *Turn off the TV and go to bed!* The most common slumber thief is television, so keep them out of bedrooms. Other culprits include napping too late or too long, reading or watching something stimulating before bed, drinking soda or coffee in the evening. It is necessary to wind down before you lie down.

❑ *"But I have promises to keep.* And miles to go before I sleep." However, even the wise Robert Frost would probably agree that a fifteen-minute rest can often increase an individual's efficiency and productivity. Sleep is a valuable investment of time.

Habits p. 31, Relaxation p. 73, Time Management p. 157

"If spanking worked, we'd only have to do it once."

Nancy Samalin, 1991

Abuse

❏ *Don't get used to abuse.* Abuse is the showing of disrespect toward any living thing. No matter what sex, age, or culture, abuse of any kind is wrong. Children must be explicitly taught how to recognize emotional, physical, sexual, or neglectful mistreatment and who to talk to for help.

❏ *Low-impact abuse.* Degrading speech and behavior may not result in black eyes. But it can brutally damage an individual's self-esteem, which influences every aspect of life from eating habits to friendships. Do what you need to do to boost your own self-worth so you can offer your sincere support to the ones you love.

❏ *Communication is key.* Physical harm is not acceptable. However, neither are the vicious words and behaviors that often provoke violence. Trace an incident back to the first *words* thrown, not just the first punch. Then teach *both* victims how to more effectively express and manage their feelings.

❏ *Stop the cycle.* If you are a man, woman, teenager, or child whose life is controlled by fear or intense anger, help is available. Call your local hospital, school, or church for assistance. Break the chain reaction of domestic abuse and your children's children will thank you.

Confidence p. 77, Disagreement p. 93, Anger p. 105

*"They are much pitied who have not
been given a taste for nature in early life."*

Jane Austen, 1814

Nature

❑ *Beware:* The dreaded "garage-office-garage" syndrome is epidemic in some households. Take five minutes each day to appreciate crisp winter air, look at the stars, or walk barefoot in the grass so you can avoid this monotonous fate. Nature is all around us, and no specialized gear or planning is necessary to be a part of it.

❑ *Survival of the fittest.* Rock-solid relationships are built on shared experiences, not common television time. Go camping, hiking, canoeing, fishing, snorkeling, skiing, or ice skating with friends and family members because when memories are made outdoors, they survive.

❑ *Nature is not always nice.* Wild animals will defend themselves if they feel threatened. The silent power of water currents can easily be underestimated. Severe weather should be taken seriously. Humans who respect the power of nature stay alive to enjoy it.

❑ *Reusing and recycling* are great ways to do your part in the worldwide effort to condense waste. However, reducing the amount of "stuff" you buy in the first place saves money and conserves resources. A small stone thrown into a big pond still makes a ripple.

Generosity p. 23, Safety p. 41, Television p. 109

"Biology is the least of what makes someone a mother."

Oprah Winfrey, 1988

Pregnancy

❑ *We have the right to choose.* When a woman *chooses* to become sexually active, she decides to possibly become pregnant. When a man *chooses* to become sexually active, he decides to possibly cause a pregnancy. From there, taking responsibility for your behavior is not necessarily the easy choice, but it is the right one.

❑ *Mistakes are for math,* not babies. An unplanned pregnancy can range from devastating to inconvenient depending on the situation of the parents. Even when married, couples should use reliable forms of birth control until they feel well prepared to have a child. Babies should be considered a blessing from the beginning.

❑ *Order of operations.* Just as the children's tune goes, "first comes love, then comes marriage, then comes a babe in the baby carriage." Too many people seem to forget what may sound obvious. A husband and wife should feel physically, emotionally, and financially stable *before* they have a baby.

❑ *Are you expecting?* Every woman's body goes through extreme changes during pregnancy. You can decide to focus on the fluttering feeling when the baby is kicking or the dull ache in your lower back as the baby grows. When it comes to enjoying a pregnancy, often you get what you are expecting.

Abstinence p. 11, Married Sex p. 67, Parenthood p. 103

*"At the worst, a house unkept
cannot be so distressing as a life unlived."*

Rose Macaulay, 1926

Cleanliness

❑ *Speed cleaning.* Whether you are aiming to clean the house, the garage, or the neighborhood, anticipation and procrastination can take far longer than the actual task. So set a specific goal and a timer, turn on motivating music, and let the machine answer the phone. Go!

❑ *Get dirty!* Do you think a steaming massage shower with scented shampoo and soft music sounds nice? Go run around in the yard with the dog or work up a great sweat at the gym and then try it! Nothing makes getting cleaned up feel better than getting good and dirty.

❑ *Regular hand washing is important,* but perpetual scouring, disinfecting, and sterilizing can actually prevent the development of healthy immunities, which combat illness naturally. A point to think about, if you find that you are cleaning more than you are playing.

❑ *Healthy teeth and gums* often go unappreciated until there is a problem. Regular professional cleaning, brushing and flossing can prevent cavities, gingivitis, and even bad breath. You may as well do it, because the biting pain of a toothache will bring the toughest case of denial into the dentist's office.

Habits p. 31, Nature p. 55, Disease p. 61

"As I see it, every day you do one of two things; build health or produce disease in yourself."

Adella Davis, 1954

Disease

❑ *It can't happen to me.* Do not be naïve; of course "it" can happen to you. No matter how young, wealthy, or famous, all people are susceptible to disease. Physical health is like the air we breathe; it is easy to take it for granted until it starts to disappear, then it is difficult to think about anything else.

❑ *An ounce of prevention.* Wash your hands with soap before eating. Do not smoke. Drink three tall glasses of water a day. Get yearly physical exams and tests. Sleep six to eight hours a night. Eat healthy foods. Do not have sex outside of marriage. Take vitamins daily. Exercise regularly.

❑ *A pound of cure.* Get a second opinion because doctors *can* make mistakes. Do your own research about an illness and various treatments. Look for natural solutions, such as vitamin supplements and lifestyle changes, whenever possible. And if medication is necessary, follow directions precisely.

❑ *What comes around goes around.* Fighting disease is not a one-person battle. Raise awareness, support scientific research, donate blood, immunize children, and bring a moment of happiness to those who are ill. Kindness is contagious; pass it around.

Abstinence p. 11, Habits p. 31, Cleanliness p. 59

*"Research tells us that fourteen
out of any ten individuals like chocolate."*

Sandra Boynton, 1982

Diet and Nutrition

❑ *It's a habit, not a diet.* Only healthy groceries come in the house. Snack on fruits, vegetables, and nuts. Sit down to eat. Drink milk instead of soda. Use salt and butter lightly. Develop a taste for whole wheat bread. Skip the fast food. Eat smaller portions. Bake foods instead of frying them. Eat slowly. Drink water.

❑ *Immediate gratification* can go to your hips. It is easier to approach eating as simply a means of sustaining health when you remember the fact that ten minutes after indulging in a sinful dessert you will no longer taste it. Shift your focus from short term pleasures to long term health and you will enjoy success.

❑ *Don't starve yourself*, as hunger greatly increases your chances of eating too much too fast. Instead, eat smaller portions more often. If hunger sensations cannot be avoided, drink two tall glasses of milk *before* you eat. You will then feel "full" after one serving.

❑ *Are you really hungry?* If you are depressed, talk to a friend or a counselor. If you are bored, do something active like exercise. If you are watching television or a movie, chew gum. If you are socializing, go dancing, bowling, or golfing. If you are tired, take a rest. If you are hungry, eat a healthy meal.

Habits p. 31, Exercise p. 39, Disease p. 61

"Do not take life too seriously."
"Do not take death too seriously."

Elaine St. James

Death

❑ *Do it today.* Death is the *only* absolute in every human life; however, it is often the single experience for which we feel least prepared. So, tell your family you love them, show them you love them, tell them you love them, and show them you love them—every day.

❑ *Believe in Heaven.* This may be the single most powerful thing each of us can do to cope with the mysteries of death. Know within your heart of hearts that there is an existence beyond what we know, with grace and love that we cannot comprehend.

❑ *Celebrate their life.* When a loved one dies, acknowledge feelings of denial, anger, and sadness with this goal in mind; to gradually allow pleasant memories to overcome painful emotions. With time, you *can* choose to smile through the tears.

❑ *There is more to live for.* No man is an island unto himself. Everything we do affects other humans as much as everything we don't do. Be cautious to not let a reasonable time of grief become extended self-pity. There are so many who need you alive.

Love p. 9, Depression p. 49, Help p. 101

"Sex is hardly ever just about sex."

Shirley MacLaine, 1985

Married Sex

❑ *Pillow talk should be soft hearted.* A mature sexual relationship between two married people is an evolving experience, so change should be expected. Hormones, sleep needs, self-esteem, physical health, and emotional maturity all effect this relationship. Speak with gentle honesty and listen compassionately.

❑ *The kitchen connection* is critical. The conversation that goes on at the dinner table or anywhere else in the house sets the tone for the rest of the evening. When couples can talk, laugh, and even disagree in a respectful and admiring way, intimacy comes more easily. Shared thoughts are at least as important as shaved legs.

❑ *Truth or dare.* I dare the media to tell the TRUTH about what to expect in a healthy sexual relationship. Time to learn, effort to please, absolute commitment, emotional connection. This kind of relationship is so different from those seen on television and in movies, it should be called by another word. Love.

❑ *The icing on the cake.* Physical intimacy is *one* of a long list of ways happily married couples show their love for one another. Therefore, if necessary, you could remove any one element (even sex) and a strong bond would remain. Couples who share dreams and activities together enjoy many anniversary cakes-with icing!

Responsibility p. 7, Pregnancy p. 57, Parenthood p. 103

"What you risk reveals what you value."

Jeanette Winterson, 1992

Emergency Skills

❑ *Human instinct* can supersede age, gender, and even skill level. Learn to listen to your own common sense to help *avoid* dangerous situations. When faced with a problem, stay calm and react with a cool head. Recognize the power adrenaline gives you and use it! You are alert. You are quick. You are resourceful.

❑ *Minimal training builds smart reflexes.* Instead of jumping in the water to save a frenzied swimmer, a prepared individual would grab a long stick and pull them in. A child who is *taught* to run, scream, and tell when approached by a suspicious stranger will react instead of freeze in fear. Create a future hero; learn emergency skills today.

❑ *CALL 911.* Keep your name and current address posted in a visible location for baby-sitters, visitors, and yourself, as even you may forget if you are frightened. Speak as clearly as possible and STAY ON THE PHONE! Emergency phone attendants can trace a call if the phone connection is long enough, so do not hang up too soon.

❑ *Swimming is a must.* Most sports and extracurricular activities should be based on the individual interests of the young person. However, learning how to swim and be safe near water is a responsibility that should be taken seriously by children, teenagers and adults. Have fun; learn how to swim safely.

Habits p. 31, Safety p. 41, Driving p. 47

"You must do the thing you think you cannot do."

Eleanor Roosevelt, 1960

Disability

❑ *A handicap is not a disability* until it keeps you from doing something you want to do. If your fear of heights keeps you from climbing a mountain, "fear" is your disability. Find a way to achieve your dreams and strength of character becomes your *ability*.

❑ *No sympathy necessary*. Lend a hand to those who want to overcome a disability. Empower people who are in need of courage and a sense of independence. And when an individual works hard to learn how to manage everyday life with a handicap, give them nothing less than your respect.

❑ *Helen Keller* never recovered her sight, hearing, or speech after she was stricken by a fever at the age of nineteen months in 1881. Seven years later, a tutor named Ann Sullivan rescued Helen from her torturous silence. Helen went on to live a life that inspired the world. Success breeds success for teachers and learners. Look for it.

❑ *You are not alone*. Whether you are an individual struggling to overcome a handicap or an extraordinary person assisting someone else, do not isolate yourself. There are others like you. Seek the company, insights, and emotional support that people and organizations have to offer.

Problem Solving p. 97, Help p. 101, Learning Style p. 129

"In a society that judges self-worth on productivity, it's no wonder we fall prey to the misconception that the more we do, the more we're worth."

Ellen Sue Stern, 1988

Relaxation

❑ *Work hard to relax.* Nothing makes downtime sweeter than hard work. Whether a person is two, thirty-two, or ninety-two years old, participating in meaningful activity is paramount. So, go ahead, work your buns off and then sit them down and put your feet up.

❑ *Take your leisure time seriously.* In an age where a decorative calendar can become a silent dictator, it may be necessary to literally schedule relaxation time (not "TV time") for you and your family on weekdays and weekends. Give it the same respect as a dental appointment or a business meeting, as the return is often greater.

❑ *Vacation and relaxation are not always synonymous.* Too often planning, packing, traveling, touring, paying, returning, and laundering can be exhausting rather than relaxing. Learning how to unwind in simple ways increases the chances of it actually happening. Think about it while taking a leisurely walk tonight.

❑ *There is no "mall" in holiday.* Mother's Day, Valentine's Day, Easter, and especially Christmas, celebrate people and events far more significant than what can be found at JCPenney's. Let *one* special family tradition reflect the true meaning of a holiday, and holidays will begin meaning more to you.

Happiness p. 5, Nature p. 55, Time Management p. 157

Chapter 3

Communication

*"I'm five-feet-four,
but I always feel six-foot-one, tall and strong."*

Yvette Mimieux, 1979

Confidence

❑ *Life-defining personal characteristic.* Self-esteem, or lack thereof, directly affects the grades you achieve in school, the friends you have, the career you pursue, the person you marry, and the parent you become. Those who invest time, energy and money in developing a strong sense of self-confidence profit exponentially.

❑ *Confidence begins with kindness.* Countless numbers of people have found assistance with self-reliance issues through the use of communication books, tapes, classes, etc. Others have benefited from pursuing personal interests or professional counseling. However, nothing tops the sincere words of support and a pat on the back from someone you care about.

❑ *Confident is not "cocky."* True confidence is a quiet satisfaction with yourself that can be sensed by children, adults, and even animals in a matter of seconds. Often, those who are self-absorbed or boastful are seen as less sure of themselves. Know your worth and others will, too.

❑ *Independence starts with "I".* Do not push others away, but do invite safe opportunities to practice self-reliance. A confident person can eat alone, sit up tall, and smile at a friendly face across the room. Confidence is courage. And courage is doing something even though you may be afraid.

Respect p. 25, Beauty p. 29, Presentation p. 79

"Your clothes speak even before you do."

Jacqueline Murray, 1989

Presentation

❏ *It may not be right, but it is reality.* Most people pass hard judgment on a new face within approximately five seconds. Therefore, learn the role you want to play before you are on stage. If you are a rising star then walk like one, talk like one, dress like one, and you are halfway there.

❏ *Wanted: friendly, but assertive!* If you were raised to be sweet and submissive, it is time to make a conscientious effort to save your smiles, limit your apologies, and speak with a confident voice. Gracefully demand the respect you deserve from friends, family, colleagues, and yourself.

❏ *Don't be a clone.* People should be proud of their individuality. However, shaving your head, getting tattoos, and piercing anything with skin categorizes you as much as driving a red convertible with dark sunglasses and bleached hair. Finding subtle ways to make a unique statement can make you *really* stand out in a crowd.

❏ *Add a smile to your style.* No amount of makeup, hair styling, or expensive clothes can replace a sincere, confident smile. Want to make a good impression on a date, an interview, at home, or even on the telephone? Let your smile shine through your eyes and in your voice. It's not just for cameras any more!

Beauty p. 29, Marketing p. 81, Body Language p. 87

"Which is worse;
the wide diffusion of things that are not true,
or the suppression of things that are true?"

Harriet Martineau, 1837

Marketing

❑ *Sex sells.* Consumers should be knowledgeable about the most effective techniques used by creative advertisers. The most common include: repetition, building a sense of dissatisfaction, marked-up pricing for a "sale," cute kids, and sexy women. Recognizing these often subtle but seductive marketing tools will help resist them.

❑ *Do not underestimate the power of the media.* Those relatively few products and causes that harness media strength hold much of our society in the palms of their hands. However, on an individual level the control is yours. Before you "buy" it, ask yourself what are they are really selling and why.

❑ *Buying is not bad.* In fact, it is the backbone of any economy based on capitalism. However, when people are drawn into consistently spending beyond their means, the economic upturn is short-lived. When reality sets in and bills must be paid, businesses and consumers suffer. Avoid depression; be a smart shopper.

❑ *If the shoe fits, use it.* The right to make use of successful marketing techniques is not reserved by professional advertising agencies. When you need to grab the attention of an audience, use inspirational music, dramatic photography, entertaining speakers, and attractive displays to promote your cause—it works.

Beauty p. 29, Television p. 109, Finances p. 121

"Silence is one of the great arts of conversation."

Hannah More, 1777

Conversation

❑ *Essential expressions:* The first is, "Thank you." The second is, "I'm sorry." Though simple, these two phrases may be the most powerful in the English language. When these words are spoken with sincerity, eye contact, and the listener's name, few can resist returning warm feelings toward the speaker.

❑ *Give and take.* Practice finding common areas of interest in conversation. One-word answers leave a listener dangling with little to grasp on to. Personal documentaries leave them looking for an escape. Keep the discussion relevant to your partner, and you will leave them wanting more.

❑ *Do your homework!* Before attending a dinner party, speaking to someone important on the telephone, or going on a hot date, make a list! Think about whom you will be speaking with and what would be appropriate and interesting to talk about. A little list can make a conversation go a long way.

❑ *Active listeners take time.* Time to observe body language. Time to repeat what they heard to confirm understanding. Time to sift through details to get at the heart of what is being said. Time to ask pertinent questions to clarify information. And when the time comes for them to speak, others listen.

Speaking p. 85, Body Language p. 87, Disagreement p. 93

"It makes a great difference to a speaker whether he has something to say, or has to say something."

Nellie L. McClung, 1945

Public Speaking

❏ *Oral language proficiency* is a smart priority. Although reading and writing skills are important, learning how to express your thoughts verbally is paramount. Therefore, whether you are speaking to an audience of two or twenty-two, look for opportunities to practice presenting your ideas effectively.

❏ *Organization: keep it simple.* A strong introduction will grab the audience's attention, the body of an effective presentation shares information in a logical format, and the conclusion reviews the main points covered. Voice inflection, examples, and humor can add spark, but these three elements of organization create clarity.

❏ *Eye contact is essential.* Practice in front of a mirror or video camera numerous times. Use briefly written notes on a few cards to avoid "reading" your presentation. Memorize the introduction and conclusion. The audience may not remember your specific words, but maintain good eye contact and they *will* remember your sincerity.

❏ *People listen with their eyes* so making use of well-prepared props and visual aids can enhance comprehension, keep the speech focused, and make the material memorable. However, do not let them distract from the eyes or voice of the speaker. And when using technical equipment, make sure it is in working order *before* the presentation.

Presentation p. 79, Body Language p. 87, Music p. 107

"What you do speaks so loud
I cannot hear the words you say."

Ralph Waldo Emerson

Body Language

❑ *Voices speak; body language screams.* Upright posture and direct eye contact communicates interest and self-assurance. Crossing your arms in front of your body or directing your shoulders away from a subject can express distaste. Increase your awareness of what you are saying *before* you open your mouth and then—smile.

❑ *The power of touch.* Physical contact can enhance or weaken a relationship in a second! A firm handshake displays confidence. A touch on the arm while telling a story can create a special connection between people or be inappropriately suggestive. Be aware of the power of touch and use it wisely.

❑ *To get the part, you have to play the part.* Whether traveling overseas, to another town, or upstairs to the executive suite, customs vary. To know what is expected, ask directly and/or observe an "expert" closely. People are most comfortable with those who walk and talk the way they do.

❑ *Manners are like electricity*, they often go unnoticed until they are missing. At a job interview, will saying "excuse me" and "thank you" secure the job? Perhaps not. However, the absence of basic etiquette *will* likely jeopardize it. So, whether Mom is there or not, keep your elbows off the table and chew with your mouth closed!

Confidence p. 77, Presentation p. 79, Conversation p. 83

"Loneliness is black coffee and late-night television;
solitude is herb tea and soft music."

Pearl Cleage, 1993

Loneliness

❑ *A time to talk.* To accommodate shyness in a child is to create an adult who will suffer the consequences of poor communication skills. Friendships, career opportunities, and personal image hinge upon the ability to communicate effectively. Shyness can be overcome, one successful word at a time.

❑ *Alone in a crowded room.* Loneliness can be a self-fulfilling prophecy. The more one dwells on feeling isolated, the more his or her body language pushes others away. Take the focus off yourself by volunteering for someone else in need and then take active steps to improve your self-image (exercise, education, etc.) When you like you, others will, too.

❑ *Looking for love* in all the right places. Those who *actively* pursue relationships in logical places find them. First, consider what kind of individual you are looking for. Then, ask yourself, "Where is that kind of person likely to be found?" School, church, clubs, sporting events, outdoor activities, etc. Then be there—often.

❑ *"Time out"* should not be considered a punishment. Children learn to fear and dislike time alone when it is used as a form of negative discipline. Teach them that taking a few minutes of quiet, individual time is a smart and reasonable option for people of all ages. "Take five" and feel refreshed.

Generosity p. 23, Dating p. 95, Time Management p. 157

"Friends are the family we choose for ourselves."

Edna Buchanan, 1995

Friendship

❏ *Make your goals*, then make your friends. Surround your-self by those you aspire to be like. If you hang out with people who play sports, respect their families, value educa-tion, and enjoy life, it is likely that you will, too. Of course, the opposite is also true. Shared goals create strong rela-tionships.

❏ *Friendship is like aspirin.* While two hours together may make you feel terrific, ten may make you sick. Go for qual-ity with the friends you choose and the time you spend with them. Boredom can quickly lead to arguments and irresponsible behavior. So, just take two and call them in the morning.

❏ *Beware of the "friendship of convenience."* It is good to know and be cordial toward neighbors and peers at school and work, but be wary of serious relationships. They may be built on mutual location, instead of common values and interests. You may find yourself becoming someone else's idea of a friend.

❏ *Peer pressure* is a natural result of living in a society of peo-ple. It can have positive or negative effects on individuals of any age. The trick is to be aware of its influence on you and maintain ultimate authority over what you say and do. Go ahead, everybody's doing it!

Respect p. 25, Confidence p. 77, Loneliness p. 89

"Reconciliation is more beautiful than victory."

Violeta Barrios de Chamorro, 1929

Disagreement

❑ *Four commandments of arguing*: Thou shall NOT: dig up old dirt, generalize, resort to name calling, or walk away. Memorize these commandments and share them with the ones you care for most; they are probably the ones with whom you argue. Note: Physical contact of any type is not a feature of arguing, see "abuse."

❑ *No extremes necessary.* Constant nagging and the "silent treatment" are immature forms of communication. Skilled conversationalists balance speaking with listening, apologizing with forgiving, and compromise with persistence. Choose your battles wisely and then actively set about making an adversary your ally.

❑ *Compromise is a learned skill,* not an instinctive habit. It takes time, imagination, and willingness to share power. Time to consider the argument objectively from both sides. Imagination to brainstorm for ideas that will meet the needs of both parties. Share power by allowing two winners, opposed to wanting to see the other person lose.

❑ *The bigger, the better.* It takes a "big" person to admit when they are wrong. And an even "bigger" person to resist gloating. So, whenever possible, admit a mistake, forgive a mistake, and move on. Arguing is one skill where the better you get at it, the less you'll do it.

Cooperation p. 15, Abuse p. 53, Anger p. 105

*"In real love you want the other person's good.
In romantic love you want the other person."*

Margaret Anderson, 1953

Dating

❑ *The dating game.* 15-20 years old: Don't get too serious, go out in groups, start to learn about the way the opposite sex thinks. 20-30: Look for the real thing, go out as a couple, learn how a successful relationship works. 30+: Look at yourself; is there something you need to change to attract the kind of person you are interested in?

❑ *Dating is not sex and sex is not dating.* No matter your age, nothing complicates dating faster than becoming sexually involved. A relationship that was once spontaneous and fun loving can overnight become self-conscious and jealous. Just K.I.S.S! Keep it simple, sweethearts.

❑ *Keep it alive, keep it active.* Take a walk in the park, attend a concert, go for a bike ride, visit a museum, bake a cake, volunteer together, go to a dance, or exercise together. Meaningful memories are made from living life, not watching movies of other people pretending to.

❑ *Dating doesn't stop* when you get married. Well, at least with your spouse! Get rid of your satellite dish and commit the time and money you would have spent watching television to nightly conversation and a "hot date" once a month. The critical nature of this investment multiplies with the birth of each child.

Abstinence p. 11, Loneliness p. 89, Marriage p. 99

"Never be afraid to sit a while and think."

Countess of Blessington, 1839

Problem Solving

❑ *Define the problem:* What is the essence of the dilemma? Where did the problem originate? Who are the key people involved? The more focused these answers are, the better equipped one is to create solutions. Strive to cure the underlying cause of the problem rather than merely address the symptoms.

❑ *List your options:* Use creativity, logic, and a specific goal to devise a list of feasible solutions to the problem. For each choice, consider possible positive and negative results. Do not forget to include "no action necessary" or a personal "change in attitude" as potential responses.

❑ *Take action:* In an emergency situation a person can problem solve in the blink of an eye. Other challenges allow time for more in-depth consideration. In either case, however, nothing will change without action, from you or someone else. Go with your gut feeling and make a good thing happen.

❑ *Does your life resemble daytime television?* The human brain craves stimulation. If individuals do not have positive excitement, they will unconsciously create negative conflict to spice things up. Therefore, learn to feel satisfied with healthy activities and relationships and you will be more apt to resist the hurtful ones.

Cooperation p. 15, Marriage p. 99, Research p. 131

*"A great marriage is not so much finding the right person
as being the right person."*

Marabel Morgan, 1973

Marriage

❑ *You can buff the edges,* but do not plan to change the mold. The fundamental make up of a person's character is well defined by age five. Therefore, if you do not like what you see at eighteen or twenty-five, look somewhere else! Only *rare* personal dedication and assistance can make a prince, or princess, out of a toad.

❑ *Marry someone you like.* The person you choose to spend your life with should be a person you would enjoy spending the day with. Do you have common life goals, similar hobbies or interests, family backgrounds, and personal values? "I like you" can sometimes be a stronger endearment than "I love you."

❑ *Your spouse must be #1.* Before extended family; yes, even Mom. Before friends; "best" ones included. Before your career; even though it may have preceded your relationship. Even before children; their happiness is directly proportional to yours. When spouses sense that their time and love is valued above all others, it creates a willingness to share.

❑ *They lived happily ever after,* but it took work! The marriage of two people with different upbringings and expectations is going to take effort. Plan for it. Most situations can be remedied through honest communication and forgiveness, but get professional help *early* if it is necessary.

Cooperation p. 15, Dating p. 95, Problem Solving p. 97

*"Give him a fish and he will eat for a day.
Teach him to fish and he can eat for a lifetime."*

Unknown

Help

❑ *Get professional help early.* Most people need it at some point in their life, whether it is for a marital, parenting, or personal dilemma. Some get help, others get divorced. Some get help, others mistreat their children. Some get help, others continue addictive behaviors. Get help and others will respect you.

❑ *Help is just around the corner:* Family, friends, self-help books, phone book, hospitals, churches, libraries, schools, police station, the Internet, doctor's office, insurance companies, some radio and television talk shows. Actively pursue sources that will work for you and then give their recommendations time and practice.

❑ *Help is education, not just charity.* Teaching an individual how to handle a problem independently is empowering. Creating a long-term situation where they feel dependent upon the welfare of others is demeaning. A donation may help someone to his or her feet, but education will get them walking.

❑ *Help yourself.* Actively participate in making your success a reality by asking questions and practicing techniques. It is far easier to assist people who pull their own weight, than those who expect to be carried. Attitude, it may not be everything, but it is a lot.

Responsibility p. 7, Generosity p. 23, Career p. 125

"A good example has twice the value of good advice."

Unknown

Parenthood

❏ *To work or not to work,* that is the question for many supplementary wage earners. Meaningful part-time employment or volunteer work can provide a sense of accomplishment critical in maintaining a positive outlook toward parenthood. Remove the paycheck from the equation and do what creates a happy family.

❏ *Disciplined parents:* Predict and prevent situations where punishment may become necessary. Clearly state expectations and reasonable consequences. Do not give warnings; follow through with an appropriate response *every* time a rule is broken. ALWAYS show respect for a child's feelings and body.

❏ *Time is an expensive gift.* No amount of designer clothes, costly vacations, fancy cars, or private schooling will replace quality time spent with children and teenagers. Parents who routinely create time to throw a ball, take a walk, listen to a story, read a book, or play a game with each of their children deserve a "thank you."

❏ *The golden rule of parenthood.* Do unto them as you would have them do unto you—because they will! When teaching a young person the importance of punctuality, for example, a parent should be on time to pick them up from school. Effective educators show first and then tell.

Marriage p. 99, Help p. 101, Family p. 115

"Anger is a signal, and one worth listening to."

Harriet Lerner, 1985

Anger

❑ *Before you blow:* Are you hungry? Are you tired? Are you bored? Are you stressed? Whether you are four or forty-four, human beings become more irritable when basic needs are not met. Next time you are feeling frustrated, ask yourself these four questions. A well-timed snack may extinguish a burning fuse.

❑ *Be prepared.* Feelings of anger and frustration usually strike when we are feeling physically or emotionally weakened. Successful communicators have appropriate responses in mind that take the edge off their temper without harming themselves or others. Go for a fast walk instead of a fast drive.

❑ *Forgiveness is not necessarily friendship.* It takes an incredible amount of energy to maintain feelings of revenge, irritation, and hate. Therefore, take action to prevent the situation from happening again, forgive the incident, and let it go. This does not mean befriend someone who hurts you. Forgiveness simply enables you to move on.

❑ *Anger, like happiness, is contagious.* If you surround yourself with frustrated people, listen to aggressive music, watch violent movies, etc., you will probably catch it. If you grew up in an angry household, it is going to take effort and probably outside assistance to prevent the cycle from continuing. You can decide to change.

Abuse p. 53, Conversation p. 83, Disagreement p. 93

"Nothing recalls the past like music."

Madame de Stael, 1807

Music

❑ *Finding your voice.* Listen to your voice on the answering machine. Is it thin and weak or strong and commanding? Experiment and practice molding your singing and speaking voice into the effective communication tool it can be. Less than 2% of the population are actually "tone deaf," most are just tone shy.

❑ *Changing the station* can change your mood. Music can evoke sorrow, pride, anger, joy, fear, or serenity faster than many actions or words. If you want to have a great workout, create a party atmosphere, or relax after a busy day, choose the right music and you'll be moving in the right direction.

❑ *Do you want to dance?* Yes! Children learn how to coordinate their bodies and develop a sense of rhythm. Teenagers engage socially at dances, rather than hang out in parking lots. Adults have an active hobby they can pursue *with* their spouse. Boys and girls, guys and gals, men and women should learn how to dance.

❑ *Marching to a different beat.* Band and orchestra instruments can provide a wonderful sense of social belonging and achievement, especially during school years. Guitar, piano, and singing instruction can be beneficial long after graduation. Ask yourself *why* you want to play *what* you want to play.

Talents p. 33, Relaxation p. 73, Artistic Ability p. 111

*"Television has opened many doors—
mostly on refrigerators."*

Mary Waldrip, 1989

Television

❑ *Prime time.* Television can be an extraordinarily effective means of mass communication. It can also be an excellent tool for education or pure entertainment. So, *sit down* and enjoy some quality television. Then...get up and turn it off.

❑ *Watch what they watch.* "Bad guys" do not target children nearly as often as advertising campaigns do. Unfortunately, the results can be similarly damaging. Violent movies, books, video games, music, and television have assisted in creating a population of young people who crave aggression.

❑ *If you don't like it, don't watch it.* Who would ever admit they really enjoy hearing about gruesome murder, child abuse, and the unspeakable evils of war? Do you? Watching violence on television, movies, or even on the "news" does not prevent it. There is a fine line between being informed and being entertained.

❑ *Wean yourself today.* The average American household has the television on for 7½ hours a day. As an alternative, turn on music for background noise, listen to news radio for current events, read a book if you are bored, provide alternate activities for children and teens. Live your life, cut the cable.

Relaxation p. 73, Marketing p. 81, Family p. 115

"Imagination is more important than knowledge."

Albert Einstein

Artistic Ability

❏ *The eye of an artist.* Learn to view the world through the eyes of an artist and it will never look the same again. Suddenly, the subtle effects of lighting, background, expression, line, and space become obvious and impor- tant. Add color to everyday life—develop your artistic ability.

❏ *The spoken crayon.* There are hundreds of techniques and materials used by artists of all types around the world. Painters may choose watercolor, oil, charcoal or pencil. Sculptors can use clay, stone, wood, ice, or wire. Photographers use a variety of film types, digital special effects, or video. Have a message? Choose a medium.

❏ *Creativity with conscience.* Art can be an incredibly effec- tive means of communication and self-expression. It can evoke deep emotions and proclaim complicated messages in seconds. Therefore, wield the power of art with care and a sense of responsibility. Just because it *can* be said does not mean it *should* be.

❏ *The starving artist.* Art does not have to be appreciated by the world for it to serve an important purpose. Creativity is unique by definition, so do not be discouraged if your work is not embraced by popular culture. If designing your masterpiece helps fill a need for you, get a job to put food on the table and then continue your passion.

Talents p. 33, Relaxation p. 73, Music p. 107

"Privacy is not something that I'm merely entitled to, it's an absolute prerequisite."

Marlon Brando, 1924

Privacy

❑ *The sanctity of privacy* is easily forgotten until your house is broken into, your purse is stolen, or items are missing from your mailbox. Privacy is an essential freedom that should be given to all people who use their space and abilities to contribute to society in a positive way.

❑ *Freedom from the press.* Those who envy the beauty and perceived glamour of celebrity life need to look beyond the headlines and airbrushed photographs. Ironically, when individuals reach the stardom they have worked so hard to achieve, they often want nothing more than animosity and a sense of normalcy.

❑ *Be lord of your ring.* Protecting your privacy means more than pulling your shades at night and never displaying personal information on a website. It means creating a virtual ring around yourself and those you love. And then taking caution with whom you let into your personal space-physically, emotionally, and financially.

❑ *Sad secrets exposed.* There are times when it is necessary to bring a private situation to light in an effort to improve it. However, if a news source is going to take it upon themselves to report a problem they *must* follow through by sharing help resources and possible solutions. Otherwise, the gesture is quickly reduced to simple gossip.

Loneliness p. 89, Safety p. 41, Friendship p. 91

"An ounce of blood is worth a pound of friendship."

Spanish proverb

Family

❑ *Family first.* The number of hours in a day are like the Earth's water supply, there is a finite amount of each. You can only give time to one area by taking it from another. For that reason, *before* working overtime, joining another committee, or starting a movie, spend time doing something meaningful with your family first!

❑ *Dinnertime is sacred.* Schedule soccer practice and scout meetings around it. Turn off the television and the telephone ringer. Sit at the table *together*, take a moment to give thanks, practice gracious table manners, and allow only pleasant conversation. The more undivided attention shared by a family, the less divided it becomes.

❑ *Productive families resemble an effective business.* Parents play a leadership role while listening closely and valuing the insights of their dependents. Spouses manage their time wisely by clearly defining their responsibilities. Siblings are taught to be friends and support each other whenever possible.

❑ *Too broken to mend.* If you come from a deeply dysfunctional family, there is a point where you have to leave them behind to move ahead. Seek relationships from the type of household you aspire to create. Expect hard work in developing new habits and your family can become a model to others.

Love p. 9, Cooperation p. 15, Marriage p. 99

Chapter 4

Academic Skills

"The great aim of education is not knowledge but action."

Unknown

Education

❑ *#1 Teach personal values.* Qualities such as honesty, respect, generosity, and responsibility help people make daily decisions that will lead them in the direction of life long happiness. Character education should receive at least the same amount of time and effort devoted to academic subjects. Values are not icing, they are the cake.

❑ *#2 Teach physical health facts.* What good is a Ph.D. if you acquired AIDS while you were achieving it? When time and effort is devoted to educating individuals on specifically how they can create and protect their health-they do. Young people must be given accurate information and practice in making healthy decisions.

❑ *#3 Teach communication skills.* Between the ages of five and eighteen you spent approximately 1,600 hours learning mathematical concepts. Math is important, but communication skills are essential both personally and professionally. Some people will become mathematicians, however nearly all people will become married.

❑ *#4 Teach academic excellence.* Learning *how* to learn will bring richness to an individual for as long as they live. It will also bring wealth to their bank account, as good grades can lead to higher education, increased career opportunities, and a lifestyle of choice. Enrich the life of the ones you love, instill a love of learning.

Introduction p. 1, Spirituality p. 27, Confidence p. 77

"The safest way to double your money is to fold it over once and put it in your pocket."

Frank McKinney Hubbard

Finances

❑ *A five-year-old can tell you money is important;* it is one of the first lessons our society teaches. Unfortunately, money management skills are not necessarily included in that education. People need to learn how to save, budget, share, invest, and spend wisely. Teach your children good habits or they will learn the bad.

❑ *For every paycheck received:* 1st contribute to investment and savings accounts through automatic withdraws, 2nd pay bills (including any balance on the *one* credit card you use), 3rd set aside money for necessities (groceries, gas), 4th resist going shopping just for something to do, 5th enjoy the financial stability you have created.

❑ *Be clever, invest early.* Ms. Clever invested $1.00 at 8% interest when she was **twenty years old**. When she was sixty her investment had grown to **$24.53**. Ms. Slower invested $1.00 at 8% interest when she was **thirty years old**. When she was sixty her investment had grown to **$11.02**. Who do you want to imitate?

❑ *You cannot claim ignorance on taxes.* Every April 15th all Americans making more than a designated amount of money annually are expected to complete the appropriate forms stating they will pay or have paid a percentage of their earnings to the government. State and local taxes may also exist.

Responsibility p. 7, Organization p. 153, Insurance p. 123

"Forethought spares afterthought."

Amelia E. Barr, 1885

Insurance

❑ *Insure your care before you need it.* The value of health, home, auto, and life insurance becomes crystal clear *after* an accident. The catch is, however, you must have a financial safety net in place *before* the incident occurs. Otherwise, those involved will suffer more than emotional or physical damage.

❑ *Familiarity does not overcome liability.* A friend of fifteen years will take you to court when *her* child refuses to wear a seat belt and then is injured in an accident in *your* car. This harsh reality compels wise individuals to ensure the safety of anyone who comes near their property, including disobedient kids.

❑ *A little prevention can* equal a lot of money. Insurance companies reward customers who take steps to prevent accidents and illness from happening in the first place. The rewards of choosing not to smoke, getting good grades, and maintaining a safe driving record are more than the obvious.

❑ *Let your will be known.* If it is your wish to discontinue life support in certain circumstances, it must be documented in a "living will" *before* the occasion arises. If you have specific instructions for the care of your dependents and distribution of your estate, make it known in a legal will. Share your wishes.

Responsibility p. 7, Safety p. 4, Finances p. 121

"We make a living by what we get.
We make a life by what we give."

Winston Churchill

Career

❑ *"What do you want to be when you grow up?"* may be the most important question you ask a young person. Do not stop at kindergarten! It is never too early for an individual to explore and discover how they are going to earn their livelihood and contribute to society. However, it can be too late.

❑ *It is what you know AND whom you know.* Stocking your resume with good grades, club memberships, sporting activities, religious groups, volunteer time, achievement awards, and after-school jobs builds experience and self-esteem. Employers know this. That is why they look for them.

❑ *More than a paycheck.* Is there physical risk involved in this career? Do you have to live in a city? How much travel is involved? How much stress is there? Is continued education required? Does it offer health insurance and retirement plans? Is it "family friendly?" Do you *like* doing it? Where do you see yourself in five years, ten years? Consider the future in what you choose to do today.

❑ *Pick a career, any career...*
Communication: writer, journalist, entertainer, artist, politician
Trade school: cosmetology, auto mechanic, electrician
Education/Human services: teacher, social worker, fire fighter
Health care: physical therapist, doctor, nurse, dental hygienist
Business: human resources, salesman, manager, entrepreneur
Technology: scientist, computer programmer, graphic designer

Talent p. 33, Education p. 119, Research p. 131

*"Mathematics provides an invisible framework
that molds the more visible surface features of daily life."*

Sheila Tobias, 1987

Mathematics

❑ *Comprehension is key.* Reading is reduced to "word calling" if the student does not understand what was read. Math is limited to a "plug and chug" activity if there is no awareness of the logic behind the problem. Only when a child can explain *why* 2+2=4 do they truly have the complete answer.

❑ *Successful math students:* (1) **Visualize** the problem (either on paper or mentally) to transform abstract concepts into concrete images. (2) **Estimate** an answer. (3) **Calculate** the answer and ask themselves, "Does this answer make sense?" (4) **Arrange** this new knowledge into the "big picture" because math builds upon itself.

❑ *When will I ever use this?* Basic arithmetic: balancing a checkbook. Word problems: figuring travel time. Fractions: a "20% off" sale. Estimation: grocery shopping with a budget. Geometry: decorating your house. Statistics: current event articles. Basic algebra: baking a double batch of chocolate chip cookies.

❑ *Memorization increases fluency.* Many readers can phonetically "sound out" words. However, to do so too often disturbs the flow and comprehension of the text. Similarly, math students can follow problem-solving logic more readily when they do not have to devote concentration to basic facts. Memorize them correctly.

Career p. 125, Learning Style p. 129, Technology p. 149

"How we learn is what we learn."

Bonnie Friedman, 1993

Learning Style

❑ *Thinking about thinking. How* you know *what* you know is the essence of a concept entitled "metacognition." Significant progress is made in school, and in life, when students move beyond simply solving problems toward understanding them. Think about it. "How do you know what you know?"

❑ *You have to see it to believe it!* That is because the majority of people are visual learners. Often individuals will benefit from verbal and hands-on support. But, helping a student "see" the objective is where most effective educators place their emphasis.

❑ *A computer cannot open a box.* The same can be said for students who let a "grade" be their only goal. They may have vast potential, but two months after the test they cannot access it. Young people who learn the practical significance of specific information and are given opportunities to make use of it retain more than a grade.

❑ *To teach is to learn.* An effective way of assessing your understanding of a subject is to share it with someone else. Whether in a formal or informal setting, discuss the theme of a book you are reading, a lecture you heard, etc. Teaching can confirm a concept in one mind while introducing it to another.

Research p. 131, Memory p. 135, Note Taking p. 143

"Research is formalized curiosity.
It is poking and prying with a purpose."

Zora Neale Hurston, 1942

Research

❑ *Research is for real life*, not just book reports. Do not stop after complaining about a problem. Actively search and research possible solutions and then try them out optimistically. Those people who look like they *never* have a challenge in life have just learned how to overcome them.

❑ *Wise individuals seek the wisdom of others.* Consult parents, self-help books, medical doctors, magazines, friends, newspapers, teachers, television documentaries, the Internet, religious clergy, grandparents, guidance counselors, and/or encyclopedias. Seek and ye shall find.

❑ *Consider the source;* is their goal to advertise, entertain, or objectively inform? Do not buy into something just because it is published or an "expert" says it is so. Always question research methods and never let the creative use of statistics replace good old common sense. Search not only for an answer, but the correct answer.

❑ *A bibliography backs you up.* Finding reputable resources that support your conclusions is like having a room full of people voting for your cause. *Always* credit any book, interview, website, etc. you use to confirm your findings. It demonstrates professional courtesy, it validates your work, and it is the law!

Problem Solving p. 97, Note Taking p. 143, Tech. p. 149

"The whole of science is nothing more than a refinement of everyday thinking."

Albert Einstein, 1950

Science

❑ *It's a girl!* Our lives are directly influenced by science from the day we are born. Long before children learn to read, they become keenly aware and curious about physical and biological concepts such as gravity, hunger, and worms. Encourage them to continue asking questions and seeking answers in their scientific world.

❑ *Scientists are as creative as they are logical.* Think of the early 1900s; it took a vivid imagination to conceive an invention that would enable a human being to fly like a bird. Emphasis should be placed on both the analytical and the innovative development of young scientists. Because, sometimes "crazy" ideas can fly.

❑ *It's not just for laboratories, anymore!* Science addresses the intense human desire to understand and improve upon what is already in existence. Basic knowledge in the areas of chemistry, physics, and biology provide a solid foundation for numerous progress-oriented careers.

❑ *Three out of four forms of media recommend* believing everything they tell you. Become an educated consumer; pursue a fundamental grasp of scientific concepts and terminology. And *you* can decide what type of computer, automobile, medical test, or toothpaste is really right for you.

Career p. 125, Mathematics p. 127, Technology p. 149

*"I can never remember things
I didn't understand in the first place."*

Amy Tan, 1989

Memory

❑ *Memory is to learning as a car is to driving.* Learning how to memorize information is an ability that needs to be practiced and developed. Whether it is putting names to faces, remembering mathematical formulas, or improving basic spelling skills, those who can effectively organize and recall information learn like a Ferrari drives.

❑ *Organize information.* (1) Simplify data to only what is necessary. (2) Make sure you understand it accurately. (3) Arrange it in a logical format: alphabetical, group by type, time sequence, etc. (4) Create memory prompts: rhymes, compose jingles, associations. (5) Practice recalling.

❑ *Simulated practice is good, real use is better.* The more information is applied in an authentic, meaningful way, the more intuitive it becomes. A football video game, for example, may instill some basic rules and strategies, but it cannot compete with the skills acquired when one is actually on the field day after day.

❑ *Brain basics.* Scientists are continually revealing fascinating discoveries about the human brain. Research has shown a correlation between seclusion and the loss of memory with age. Staying socially and mentally active serves many positive purposes in life.

Simplicity p. 13, Research p. 131, Note Taking p. 143

"There is no life that does not contribute to history."

Dorthy West, 1948

History

❑ *History repeats itself.* Learning about the events, important persons, and popular trends of the past can be fascinating. However, the primary reason people must be well versed in the years that have gone by is far more fundamental. To successfully duplicate the good and overcome the bad, our society must learn from our past.

❑ *History is like any story.* The same event can be depicted from a variety of perspectives, with distinct emphasis, morals, and even outcomes. Seek out creditable sources and listen with a discerning ear. Predict where embellishments or understatements are likely to occur.

❑ *What excites you;* sports, music, food, fashion, significant events, modes of transportation, politics, dating, or family life? Throughout time, basic human nature has remained the same. Find your area of interest and get energized to learn about history. Studying the distant or recent past can be as intriguing as living the present.

❑ *The test of time.* When it comes to history, you know more than you think you do. Create two time-lines, the first examines the last two hundred years decade by decade. The second spans ancient history century by century. For each point write down at least two significant events and two important persons. So, where's Elvis?

Social Studies p. 139, Geography p. 141, Government p. 145

*"No matter who you are,
most of the people in the world are not like you."*

David Crowe, 2000

Social Studies

❏ *"I have a dream* my four little children will one day live in a nation where they will not be judged by the color of their skin but by the content of their character. I have a dream today."

        —Dr. Martin Luther King, Washington D.C., 1963

❏ *English ain't enough.* A variety of languages and dialects add vibrant color to our nation's diverse fabric. However, it is critical that all American children learn how to use grammatically correct standard English, if our intent is to offer them equal career and social opportunities.

❏ *The power of one* is dwarfed only by the power of two. Psychology is the study of how an individual mind works. When you put two of more of these minds together, the transformation is great. Sociology examines the trends of group behavior and interaction. "Learning to live" and "learning to live *together*" are different goals.

❏ *As the universe grows the earth seems to get smaller.* Anthropology, the study of various cultures, is making a leap from intriguing to essential. Investigating the intricate differences and similarities among customs can assist countries, cities, and families in an effort to move beyond coexistence toward unity.

Cooperation p. 15, History p. 137, Geography p. 141

*"Suffering makes you deep. Travel makes you broad.
In case I get my pick, I'd rather travel."*

Judith Viorst

Geography

❑ *Local geography.* Can you give accurate directions to your own house or place of business from any direction? Visualize a map in your mind, including basic cardinal directions, main roads, and distinct landmarks (not the "big tree"). Learn the most direct routes from the north, south, east and west.

❑ *"Lost" is not a good place to be found.* When receiving directions, write them as a simple bulleted list of turns, street names, and specific landmarks. Repeat them to the provider to confirm their accuracy and then look on a map to get a feel for distances. Carry the map and telephone number with you.

❑ *The cultured conversationalist.* Those who can demonstrate a basic knowledge of continents, oceans, countries, large cities, major rivers, mountain ranges, states, and capitals in casual conversation are presumed to have a well-rounded education. This knowledge also creates a context for historical and current events.

❑ *Visit your own backyard.* There are people who live in our nation's capital who have never seen the White House. And there are those who live on the coast who have never sat and watched the sun melt into the ocean. Often you do not have to go far to see wondrous things, but you do have to get up and go.

Memory p. 135, History p. 137, Social Studies p. 139

"One can live in the shadow
of an idea without grasping it."

Elizabeth Bowen, 1949

Note Taking

☐ *"Just the facts, Ma'am."* The purpose of note taking is to remind someone of the essence of information presented. Sift what the speaker is saying and record the most important points. Only direct quotes should be written verbatim, in which case the reporter should be careful to include accurate source information.

☐ *Don't write it if you don't understand it.* Note taking is an exercise that reinforces information visually and physically whether it is correct or incorrect. If you do not understand what is going on, then ask! Include personal comments and explanations in your notes to make sure you can decipher them later.

☐ *Revisit your notes.* Observe many lectures and you will find students feverishly writing pages and pages of scrupulous notes. Unfortunately, very few take the next critical step of organizing them so they can be useful. Some audience members would benefit more by putting their pencil down and just listening intently.

☐ *Not just a skill for school.* It is surprising how many people cultivate a talent in an academic or work setting, but do not carry it over into their daily lives. When you are reading or watching anything worth remembering, take notes and follow up on them. Learning opportunities happen every day; make note of them.

Simplicity p. 13, Research p. 131, Writing p. 147

*"A government can be no better than
the public opinion which sustains it."*

Franklin Delano Roosevelt

Government

❏ *More than words.* "We hold these truths to be self-evident, that all men are created equal, that they are endowed by their Creator with certain unalienable Rights, that among these are Life, Liberty and the pursuit of Happiness."
—Declaration of Independence, July 4, 1776.

❏ *Your voice is in your vote.* If you do not vote, then your views are silent (no matter how often people may hear about them). Educate yourself about the local, state, and national issues and the individuals addressing them. And on election day, put your vote where your voice is.

❏ *Party politics.* Republicans tend to maintain traditional, conservative views. Democrats gravitate toward more progressive, liberal views. Individuals who approach each issue independently with an open mind and a sense of balance bring life to the party.

❏ *Go ahead, make my day.* Our national, state, and local governments create policy that defines our daily life. So, actively support candidates, educate others on current issues, attend community meetings, participate in jury duty, write to a congressperson, or run for public office. You get points for participation.

Nationalism p. 17, Leadership p. 21, History p. 137

*"Don't write merely to be understood.
Write so that you cannot possibly be misunderstood."*

Robert Louis Stevenson, 1894

Writing

❑ *The writing process* is as old as paper itself. Thorough research and organization leads into a first draft. After rigorous self-editing, seek out objective, well-informed feedback on content and conventions. Revise, revise, revise, and finally decide you are finished working on it because writing is never perfect.

❑ *What's the point?* Effective books, movies, and even television advertisements have one thing in common: a strong thesis. The answers to who, what, where, when, why, and how questions are often creatively, but obviously, present. If readers can answer these questions about your work, your thesis is clear.

❑ *A book is judged by it's cover.* So, make sure photographs, illustrations, and diagrams are attractive and relevant. Paragraph, page length, and format should be inviting, not overwhelming. Spelling and basic grammar errors should be nonexistent. Set the stage well and the content will be evaluated from a positive perspective.

❑ *Technical writing* skills are required at most universities and places of employment. Learn how to author an outstanding research paper, journal article, business letter, instructional report, grant proposal, and oral presentation and you will be writing triumphant letters home to Mom.

Research p. 131, Note Taking p. 143, Reading p. 155

"Technology evolves so much faster than wisdom."

Jennifer Stone, 1988

Technology

❏ *State-of-the-art education* begins and ends with professional, nurturing educators and parents. Expensive equipment and materials may assist well-informed teachers in their goals, but they will not teach for them. Likewise, young children need to sit on a parent's lap when they are learning to read, not read on a "lap top."

❏ *Keep up with the kids.* Adults who stay abreast of *at least some* technological advancement encourage their children to learn skills they will need in the workplace. But it doesn't have to be painful. Look for software in a subject that interests you, such as photography. You can learn to create spectacular electronic photo albums and slideshows while developing a useful skill.

❏ *Surfing savvy.* The Internet can be a tremendous research and communication tool when used properly. When looking for information, be as specific as possible and remain meticulously focused on your purpose. When writing e-mail messages or shopping, NEVER share personal or financial information without a secure server.

❏ *Save your sanity, SAVE YOUR WORK!* Few things can bring a grown person to tears as fast as losing a month's worth of work when the computer crashes. Don't let your loved ones suffer this fate; teach them to "save" their material every two minutes, back up important documents on CD, and install antivirus software—today.

Education p. 119, Mathematician p. 127, Science p. 133

"We learn to do by doing."

John Dewey

Special Education

❑ *Face frustrations.* When neglected, a learning disability can often manifest itself as a behavior problem. It is irritating when others seemingly learn a skill with ease and you do not. Recognizing, diagnosing, and addressing a learning disorder can prevent it from becoming a personality flaw.

❑ *Independence Day.* Autonomy is the ultimate goal of education. Therefore, do *not* do for students what *they can be taught* to do for themselves. Those who are explicitly and patiently shown how to complete a task successfully and then given safe opportunities to practice their skill move toward independence.

❑ *Good teaching is good teaching.* Most of the techniques used by special education teachers work well with everyone: individual attention, realistic expectations, one specific goal for a lesson, clearly written and spoken directions, demonstration of a task, celebration of progress, and respect given to and required of all students.

❑ *Albert Einstein could not spell.* Yet, he is revered as one of the greatest minds of the twentieth century. All people have strengths and weaknesses; recognizing your own and then playing to your strong suit is nothing short of ingenious. Define yourself by your abilities, not your deficiencies.

Disability p. 71, Education p. 119, Reading p. 155

"Don't agonize. Organize"

Florence R. Kennedy

Organization

❑ *The best laid plans of mice and men* are simple and logical. Strong organizational skills are critical in finding success in education, careers, and daily life. Whether you keep meticulous files, calendars and lists, or develop a terrific memory-find a system that works for you and use it!

❑ *"If in doubt, toss it out."* Whether you are organizing data, paperwork, or a garage full of stuff, the first step is to clear away all of the nonessentials. (You may opt to set question-able items in a "to be recycled" box for a time while deciding whether or not they should be kept.) It is far easier to sustain an organizational goal when the extras are minimized.

❑ *Goal tending.* Although illegal in basketball, it is a terrific way to get things done in life. Set ONE clear, attainable goal. There may be three or four supporting objectives to assist in meeting the goal. However, one primary motive should be the focus of all efforts.

❑ *Flawless is not feasible.* There is a significant difference between seeking quality and demanding perfection. The first is a healthy expectation, while the second can become a stifling personality trait. So, expect the best efforts of yourself and those around you and then learn to feel satisfied with the results.

Simplicity p. 13, Leadership p. 21, Learning Style p. 129

*"Children are made readers
on the laps of their parents."*

Emilie Buchwald, 1994

Reading

❑ *"Verstehen sie, mein Freund?"* Unless you speak German, the words you just "read" probably do not mean very much. Speaking the words is not the same as understanding the message. So, stop often and make sure you really comprehend what you are reading. *"Do you understand, my friend?"*

❑ *Simple strategies* that effective readers use without realizing it: Look for picture or context clues, "What would make sense?" Skip a difficult word and read on, or start the sentence again. Use phonics, break the word into parts, and blend the sounds. Visualize what the words are saying while reading.

❑ *Reading is to academics as values are to life.* You *can* exist without the ability to read just as you can live without values, but there will be serious obstacles to overcome. Therefore, encouraging young people to choose books and magazines that reaffirm a positive approach to daily life addresses two high priorities at once.

❑ *Creative reading is not enough.* Just as technical writing skills are advantageous in our society, so are technical reading skills. Learning how to comprehend nonfiction material such as scientific reports and instructional text will help create a lifestyle where there is time and money available to enjoy the magic of fiction.

Education p. 119, Learning Style p. 129, Disability p. 71

"I must govern the clock, not be governed by it."

Golda Meir, 1973

Time Management

❏ *Time: Never steal from the ones you love* to pay those you do not. Even worthy causes such as school, church, work, community, and social commitments do not outweigh the importance of daily conversation and quality activities with family. Ask yourself frequently, "What use of my time will seem most important twenty years from now?"

❏ *You can say "No."* But, it takes practice. When possible, prepare a response ahead of time. Practice saying it gently, but assertively, without changing your mind. If an offer catches you off guard, buy time to think about it. Learning how to say "no" reduces the sense of burden for the times you say "yes."

❏ *The myth of "parallel processing."* Although human beings have two hands, two feet, and two eyes, we have only one brain. Get rid of distractions, determine your top priority, and focus on one thing until it is finished. In the end, a straight shooter gets more done than a juggler.

❏ *Avoid work avoidance.* Some individuals become masters at creating elaborate, time-consuming "work" to escape addressing the true issue at hand. Every day, attack your top priority first and everything else second. Keep your momentum strong and see the job through to completion. And then do not forget to celebrate!

Happiness p. 5, Simplicity p. 13, Organization p. 153

*"When I go home and turn my light off at night,
I know I did my best."*

Diana, Princess of Wales, 1996

Conclusion

You are a parent, a teacher, a mentor, or perhaps all three rolled into one. With creativity and determination, you are educating children and teenagers on how to become compassionate, health conscious, cooperative, and career savvy adults. In this way, you are providing these young people with specific tools that will send them soaring in the direction of life long happiness and success. So, relax and enjoy your work in progress. But, never underestimate the impact you are making on lives. You are a parent, teacher, or mentor, and in the eyes of a child—you are a hero. Thank you.

Shana Alexander

0-595-30507-5